DISPATCH FROM THE MOUNTAIN STATE

marc harshman

dispatch from the mountain state

poems

WEST VIRGINIA UNIVERSITY PRESS

MORGANTOWN

Copyright © 2025 by West Virginia University Press
First edition published 2025 by West Virginia University Press
Printed in the United States of America
ISBN 978-1-959000-41-9 (paperback) / ISBN 978-1-959000-42-6
(ebook)

Library of Congress Cataloging-in-Publication Data
Names: Harshman, Marc, author.
Title: Dispatch from the mountain state / Marc Harshman.
Description: First edition. | Morgantown : West Virginia University
    Press, 2025.
Identifiers: LCCN 2024038414 | ISBN 9781959000419 (paperback) |
    ISBN 9781959000426 (ebook)
Subjects: LCSH: West Virginia--Poetry. | LCGFT: Poetry.
Classification: LCC PS3608.A7839 D57 2025 | DDC 811/.6--dc23/
    eng/20240823
LC record available at https://lccn.loc.gov/2024038414

Cover and book design by Than Saffel / WVU Press
Cover image: "Squared Away" by Randi Ward, photographed at Shanholtz
Orchards in Romney, WV
For EU safety/GPSR concerns, please direct inquiries to WVUPress@
mail.wvu.edu or our physical mailing address at West Virginia University
Press / PO Box 6295 / West Virginia University / Morgantown, WV,
26508, USA.

For Maggie Anderson & Anna French

CONTENTS

THIRD

FOURTH

ACKNOWLEDGMENTS

Some of the poems in this collection have appeared previously in the following publications:

"Dispatch ... Mountain State" first appeared in the *New York Times* (November 26, 2020) and was subsequently reprinted in *Anthology of Appalachian Writers*.

"Once More Home, " "I Come to the Garden Alone," and "Back to the Garden (originally titled "Praxis") appeared in *Appalachian Review*.

"Tinnitus," "River," "Surrender," "Reminders," and "The Door Open" (originally titled "I Keep the Door Open") were published in *Still: The Journal*.

"Heart Work" appeared in *Arts: The Arts in Religious and Theological Studies*.

"Beauty and . . . ," "The Apple Trees . . . ," "Polly," "Flight Behavior," "Politics," "Late October," and "Wake," (originally titled "Grandma's Wake") were published in *Anthology of Appalachian Writers*. "Polly" was also included in the anthology *We Are Appalachia*, Mountain State Press.

"A Breach" appeared in *Now and Then: The Appalachian Magazine* (a portion later posted by Norwegian Writers' Climate Campaign).

"April 17, Romney Road" was published in *Scintilla* (Wales).

"Hunger," "Reading," and "Dancing Below the Curious Hills" were published in *Appalachian Places*.

"Taking It All On Faith" was published in *Untelling.*

"The News and the History" (originally titled "History and Headlines") was published in the anthology *Troublesome Rising: A Thousand-Year Flood in Eastern Kentucky*, University Press of Kentucky.

"Well Enough," with the title "Knowing in a Time of Fear," first appeared in an online exhibition of poetry and art posted by St. Michael's Episcopal Church, Arlington, Virginia, in 2020 and was subsequently published in *Change Seven*.

"Jackson Pollock . . ." and " I Come to the Garden . . ." were first published in *Believe What You Can*, Vandalia Press / West Virginia University.

"Some Day" first appeared in *All That Feeds Us*, Quarrier Press.

"Beech Bottom, West Virginia" was first published in *Green-Silver and Silent*, Bottom Dog Press.

"Haying" was first published in *Dark Hills of Home*, Monongahela Books, and subsequently reprinted in *The Milk House: Rural Writing Collective*.

A very special thanks to Randi Ward, not only for the loveliest of covers but also for her very close work with me on many of these poems. I thank, as well, Doug Van Gundy and Anna Egan Smucker for their friendship and their own close readings of some of these poems. And as always, unending gratitude to Cheryl for so very much.

FIRST

DISPATCH FROM THE MOUNTAIN STATE

Somewhere someone's listening to trees talk
    in a language like song,
    a song that's been going on longer than time.
Maybe.
Here we take the *maybe* with the *bad*
    and the *certain*
    alongwith everything else—nothing
    goes to waste in the heart of Appalachia.
Elsewhere behind a curtain an old man watches his
    neighbor trudge
    through snow to bring a shovel and soup.
Elsewhere a child's racing the sidewalk home
    to a dinner where Grandma
    sits in state and grace.
And somewhere someone's sleeping rough on a cold night
    and someone knows how to find this man,
    how to find a roof, blankets, soup, hope.
You see we're still holding on here just enough
    despite all we're doing wrong, holding on enough
    to give not only this man but ourselves
    enough for which to be thankful, even this,
    these little gestures that can re-birth a nation,
    reconcile not only colors
    like black and white,
    like blue and red,
    but reconcile us
    one to the other.

THE APPLE TREES WERE IN BLOSSOM

A volley of thunder, then the heavy rolling
        stock moves on, a long conversation
        of rain following and I remember, then, the loneliness
        I'd hoped to have buried deeper than I have.

Earlier, I'd seen a flock of birds
        towing up from the west
        a restless mountain of indigo clouds
        whose name you would've known.

You, who never listened to foolishness, would
        have closed each of the barn doors, latched
        the gates, lit another cigarette, and never once
        betrayed you knew the urgency I applied to all my fears.

***

There was a pet graveyard beside our old orchard:
        cats, dogs, more than one of Grandmother's canaries.
It was from one of those trees whose branches were as gnarled
        as its fruit that I fell and got this scar
        still vivid in the crease of my knuckle
        but whose moment I can never recall beyond
        knowing you named the tree a Maiden's Blush,
        almost blushing yourself to tell me so,
        shy as you were and me knowing, somehow,

beyond my years that *maiden* meant something to you
that it didn't yet mean to me.

I know now the lightning before that thunder
curled across my vision just like a scar
and had I known those birds by name
I'd never have opened my window
as I have now my heart
to what I'd thought was buried deep
beside that old orchard with its blushing trees.

RIVER

To sleep again in the house of silence,
       I will carefully fold
       my coonskin Davy Crockett
       under my pillow and reach
       for a strong story to hold
       me up over the black roar
       of Mother not speaking,
       of Father not speaking, of the tin roof
       leaking, of the closet's shit-can smelling,
       of the rotting corpse of grandmother mumbling
       next door, of the other stories whispering,
       all the million little ones
       nibbling and bullying
       until tears begin feeding
       the roar into flood.

BEECH BOTTOM, WEST VIRGINIA

Above the crumpled rise of hills west of the Ohio,
    above their shadow shoulders,
    another range lifts in the graying dark,
    an Andes-ragged accumulation of storm
    burned white against the black undertow of wind
    and there, where the river turns away south,
    the sun from some place beyond words
    leaves a palimpsest signature of light
    to limn the jagged maw where comes the night,
    and when it has gone and there are only these
    few snowflakes left within sight,
    shaken out of the drooping blanket of cold,
    I will remember the story told me long ago
    of the blizzard that came and left
    only after it had become the story it is now,
    prehistoric legend grown to gospel.

HUNGER

White peonies border the stones of the old foundation.
At the edge of the meadow peacocks fan light
    into small rainbows of flame.
You listen for the soft step of a bear,
    the black paws' chuff on the leaf litter.
An old road closes its arms
    around the forgotten, fallow fields.
Your brother will return from there in the chiffon silence
    of the afterlife, wrap you in a reassurance
    unavailable from any altar.
And here, where the sun slips into the tangle of forest,
    a barred owl is singing for his supper as he always does
    with a question much like your own.
Who'll cook for you, who'll cook for you, who'll cook for you?

THIS LIGHT

This green fills with gray, a kind of light
        that's hard to breathe if
        you've had enough of this
        day, this moment, this life
        which is exactly the problem.
We reach towards a color as if
        it might be something,
        something more
        like being with someone,
        what we call an embrace,
        perhaps, but perhaps not,
        perhaps a trap, a noose.
Sometimes, though, it will be,
        this light resembling gray,
        not what we thought at all
        but something else entirely
        and, quite probably, worse.

BLACK AND WHITE

The rabbit lawn on the north side,
       between the railroad tracks and highway,
       is deserted but for these five blackbirds
       and a limp fence of yellow tape.
The boy in jeans lay
       spread-eagled on the asphalt, unblinking
       when the sun first stepped between the bright clouds.

I began to write that I still have time to do,
       to do something, to relearn what I can do
       without his blood on my hands
       or his last words on my tongue.

But I can't. I'd be lying.
Really, there is no more time
       in this world, or the next.
I can only do this, tell you
       to count those birds again,
       give you room
       to sit down beside me and tremble
       with the silent mothers
       for whom the phone has not yet rung,
       to ball your fists

with the silent fathers
on whose door the knocks
have not yet fallen.

We don't have much time,
but we have enough
to look at those black feathers
against that white sky,
to look at black and white,
and wonder how
you and I could possibly
think the responsibility
is anyone's but our own?

READING

I was reading the lawn where it rose
       below the wind-flicker
       of shadowing leaves, reading
       for the news, and
       found it was singular
       as the best news often is.

There was a spider, not at home, but
       through its web, present,
       and within which could be
       seen a bleb of the sun
       caught inside the dew
       threaded just so
       along the falling light.

Beyond the light a woodpecker was hidden
       but with its resonant sounding board
       I could find my way to it
       without any need
       of looking for anything more
       than this one foot in front of the other.

Where I hadn't thought to look and
       what I hadn't thought to see,
       let alone name, was applause:

the applause of the long-necked mullein
and ragweed, the insidious wild garlic
and nettles whose whiskery,
breeze-driven ovation was unexpected
and undeserved.

These, then, I decided were more of the news
for which I'd been looking, another
new thing, singular
among the many and
enough to be just that,
enough.

STORM LYRICS

She still carries a satchel of tunes caught
  when the blue sky,
  split silver with lightning,
  divided the day
  into nameless infinities
  for before and after.
Slender echoes
  from that flash
  she netted
  and even now
  stitches
  this note, then this one,
  and now here, here, listen
  even I can almost find the place,
  hear that music.

SOME DAY

In the blackberry canes the sweat runs free
> and the hours disappear like shadows
> into the dusk and he remembers his mother,
> her pies, the fresh cream, the cows, the way
> the cats gathered round in the dusty light,
> eager and attentive. It was here. It is this
> allows him to breathe, memory
> the only balm in Gilead, the only bird
> still singing now her voice is gone,
> and Jenny, the children, the land gone
> to buffalo grass and slips, the outbuildings
> sagging, the money gone
> that would have fixed any of it, them, her,
> and so the pail fills up, the black glitter
> of sweetness, and he tries to reach further
> and further back where only the old memories
> have voices, a say in what he might do next.

Some days he's lucky.
Some days he brings home enough for a pie.
Some day there might be someone
> who knows what to do next.

POLLY

Let's start with a cliché, soup beans, corn bread
and a ham hock to make it right, as if
that hog had not been slaughtered behind the shed,
as if she had not had a name, believed with

us the presumption that affection was somehow
more than a next meal, more than greed for more,
but *she was a dumb beast*, could not see now,
as we do, the finer points of ethics. The gore,

though, I'd seen, the crimson and the green,
where guns, knives worked their tedious drudgery:
the muck, the smell, the dying and the death. Obscene.
Still, it is what defines us, links our mortal story

with hers, the ultimate appetite for just us,
me, to triumph over all, nothing to discuss.

TAKING IT ALL ON FAITH

The wavering striations of light
      along the yellow branch
      have yet to be painted.

A wadded ball of newsprint
      rolls down a sidewalk:
      there is a hole
      in the story somewhere.

In these ancient skies there are windows
      open just enough
      you might almost believe . . .
      if you're interested in such things.

The slow fire of green is spreading
      all that April has to give.
The branch is patient, willing to be
      forgotten, as we are not.

What we heard earlier may have been irony
      pretending to be subtle
      but was, in fact, the old rhetoric
      masquerading as something new,
      a story with a hole in its head.

Two swallows sing their duet
      writing the name of their dance
      in cursive upon the air.

It is enough, sometimes, these names
      colliding just out of reach
      of the sense
      they were born with.

DANCING BELOW THE CURIOUS HILLS

Despite the poor wages and the decline
       in morale, we kicked up our heels
       and stomped like there was better music
       than an upright and a limp tambourine.
You'd done a balloon and your smile was going
       green and soon Frank would be ready
       to climb walls with the fierce abandon
       of the already doomed.
We've been convinced for years there was no way out
       but still some nights believe spring's somewhere
       in the progression of days, that there could be
       Mendelssohn, there could be *Frühlingslied*—
       what a lazy dance of tears that would be!
But, no, what time there is shall be danced tonight
       with our own familiar drunks, and the jukebox
       when the piano dies, and the sharp crack
       of dead soldiers sparkling in the back lot
       of Roy's Rod & Gun Club will provide
       ambience, and ambivalence about it all
       will not stop our dancing for ours shall be
       a dance we dance all the way
       into the amazed morning that slips
       her rose-colored petticoats over the cold
       rocks of mountains who surrendered long ago
       and from whom we are only just now learning

to do the same knowing the stern master
will yet join us, lead our dancing in that long line
leads away from dawn into a night
where the gray rains of oblivion outlive us all.

ONCE MORE HOME

Over the hill he sees
>	a few more minutes sneak away
>	under the cover of leaf-fall and
>	turkey cackle and
>	the first wood smoke of October.

He puts dates
>	on his calendar, radiator fluid
>	in his Ford F-150, storm
>	windows in the house, fodder
>	in the shock, firewood
>	in the shed.

He even puts words
>	on his tongue
>	to hold onto time: *anniversary*,
>	*Sunday School, market day,*
>	*turn-the-clock-back day,*
>	*Thanksgiving, Christmas,*
>	says aloud *remember, remember, remember . . .*
>	but it's only *culling* and *harvest* linger.

In the graveyard
>	on his mother's stone:
>>		*but about that day or hour*
>>		*no one knows.*

But who is it knows,
>	not the hour, but the minute

when the words began to slip

not away but beyond

the ability of his tongue

to summon them

once more

home.

SECOND

ANCESTRY

Along the east rim of the cemetery I walk
       a stony ditch covered with coltsfoot
       and winter's crumpled mullein
       when beyond in the threadbare woods
       I hear an owl even though it's not
       yet dusk.
His breathy taunt of the impatient night
       seems commendable, intrigues me
       so I stop, let the silence
       he's summoned deepen.
Just when I guess he's ridden further away,
       his mumbled stutter calls again and I look
       through the thin light for the shadow within
       which he's likely standing, self-assured
       in a camouflage perfected not so much
       by color but by a proud and stoical stillness
       would rival a Trappist or Roshi
       or the feathered stones with whom
       he traces his true kin.

I COME TO THE GARDEN ALONE

So sweet the birds hush their singing . . .
Through the voice of woe . . .

> —from the hymn "In the Garden,"
> C. Austin Miles, 1912

He walked the hill
to the fence, fell
as he reached with pliers
to mend the break.

The deer had done this,
voracious, and his garden
done this, to him, and
his obsession to fix, to do,
had done this, too.

And now this, a single, slick stone
underfoot: simple,
unlucky, and no surprise
to anyone but him; still,
he needed no one, needed only
to be himself, alone, where he could deny
the years, believe against
the mounting evidence of the body.

There were already leaves,
the crescent yellow cherry leaves,
falling, burying him as if
he wished them to . . . , to do this.
He could have lain long.

Chance grows less lenient
with years, he knows, and so
allows them all, even the doc
room to pronounce and cherish
cause and effect, to preach and console,
while he plans another
ascent to the garden, another
raid on the inevitable, that last butternut
squash, that last glimpse of nurture, that last breath
of what takes him where he needs to go.

WHERE SHE LIVES

The dandelion between the porch steps
    is singing *YELLOW* at the top of its photosynthetic lungs.
Only a pair of cardinals has stopped to listen.
Meanwhile, a pool of violets slowly spreads
    down the lawn on its way to a clean river of stones.

The weather forecast so long ago eventually arrived
    and stood before me a brief minute.
The transformation was complete.

I am writing on the clouds now with tears legible
    from her window in the house with the singing dandelion.
I've never been there, but the cardinals have.
Who else could've told me about the violets
    and the way she stood
    staring out that window at dusk
    there at the end of that
    almost perfect street?

WELL ENOUGH

A fall of blossom in a sudden breeze
      and, like snow shaken from a limb,
      you shiver with what you've carried
      here from the headlines
      and bow your head.
You know you should know better.

The river sluices its cold way down the mountain
      between cracked, gray panels of stone,
      the canyon deafening with its mad roar.
The loneliness here moves the earth below you
      and you grab hold the slenderest branch,
      a whippet of cherry, and suddenly
      the whole forest is holding you up.
But, you knew this, didn't you?

On your knees amid the clutter of your study,
      a crucifix on one wall, the Stones' Hot Lips
      on another, and a window framing
      the pink haze of maples eager
      to get on with the business of spring.
Your eyes fill with something neither sad nor
      joyous, something like thanksgiving
      that someone, call Her or Him, God
      or not, but you know

there is this great listening
gathered around you.

Even as the dark mysteries of the day
assail your locked doors, your neighborhood,
your world, there is this listening much like
Julian in her cell centuries ago
hearing that convincing voice
and knowing that all will be
out of our hands but well
enough, and more
to see us to the other side
be that eternity, next year,
or simply this next second,
the one where we hear
another's heart beat just like ours.

WAKE

He keeps seeing her in the kitchen,
>   remembering, trying to place on the walls
>   what had been before, trying
>   to get past these voices, the crushing gossip
>   and sentiment he fears will cling
>   to these red, plastic chairs Grandma adored
>   because they came from her prodigal sister
>   returned from decades of bad men in California.
The Ball glass jars sit empty under the window
>   where she watched her sparrows and what once
>   must've been a rose-breasted grosbeak, her
>   *black-suited boy with the heart on his chest —*
>   took us years to figure out what she'd seen.
And you can tell me all you like
>   how wrong that description is.
And I can tell you how perfect it was for Grandma,
>   and how perfect it will remain.
I must get these people out of here.
No one allowed, the sign will say,
>   *unless you can tell*
>   *one of her stories*, and then
>   I'll know she lives
>   and that you're allowed
>   in here where I've determined
>   what must go
>   on keeping her alive.

HEADLINES

The maroon bells of the pawpaw, upturned
>   and winged enough to float
>   in this April breeze, do not ring
>   but sizzle with flies and beetles
>   busy upon a stubby clapper
>   bristling with pollen.
The doves thread their moaning whistle
>   in a white fog come down
>   with the brightening mystery
>   of clear skies to follow.
The boy on his blue bicycle is an anachronism, ball cap
>   skewed sideways on his crew cut, baseball card
>   flapping in his spokes.
An old man shuffles onto his porch, looking for his paper.

The fog lifts.

A mile away a siren goes through a tunnel
>   echoing with a story
>   I may or may not come to know, that may
>   or may not show up in the headlines.
My news is the cat leaping onto the tightrope
>   of the porch rail and the boy doffing his cap
>   and presenting a newspaper as if tribute
>   and in exchange receiving as allowance

permission to let his fingers trace
the undulate spine of a cat named Sam.
The pawpaw goes on ringing its silent beauty
and the doves scour the hillside
content to let the pawpaw speak for them.
I have no need of headlines, though wish the old man
whatever contentment he might find in them.

THE DOOR OPEN

Near Bluefield a long haul truck plunges
>through a tunnel's silence
>and a ghost of echoes follows it home.

I reject certain facts for my own pleasure.

There may be a home, there may be a sound, there may be
>some applause when that tree falls
>in that one-handed forest.

I know I have enough dandelions in my unkempt lawn
>to defy the passage of time.

A stone, big as my thumb, dislodged by a pigeon,
>rolled down my hill yesterday.

It sits on my dresser, a small monument in honor
>of every chance that's ever come my way.

I light a candle for breakfast, think about the distances
>between then and now.

I'm holding the door open for what I think may be the song
>the young woman in the grocery
>said reminded her of me.

Tonight, the moon stands tiptoe in the mackerel clouds,
>its shimmering halo pierced by Jupiter.

I can hear the stars singing that young woman's name.

I keep the door open.

I listen for those echoes to come singing through the forest.

I wait for the trucker carrying a song
        filled with enough silence to whisper the truth.
I open my arms for it, for her, open myself to the chance
        it was never her song alone, but ours.

BACK TO THE GARDEN

The soil is blackened with years of the north farm's manure.
Speckled green lifts from the unseen

    white flecks of lettuce

    seed sown weeks earlier.

Faith. Hope. Charity.
The large words of religion

    tangle with this mundane mix

    of sunshine and cowshit, rain,

    and the discipline

    to do,

    and to wait.

JACKSON POLLOCK AND THE STARLINGS, MOUNDSVILLE, WEST VIRGINIA

The painting has a life of its own. I try to let it come through.

    —Jackson Pollock

The starlings have again held their revival here.
The sidewalk below their power line pulpits
  is stippled with rose and ivory starbursts.
A few linger near yet this morning, whistling,
   as if they were unaware
   of their art, unaware
   of the limits of transcendence,
   unaware
   of the neighbors' lack of appreciation
   of mulberries, of art, of starlings with a purpose.

INSOMNIA

Somewhere beyond the trees the sky
    with its flock of clouds
    hurries home
    while the light seeps
    into every corner
    to declare night is at hand.

The white flagstones fade
    like the palimpsest sentence
    I've been following for months.

Somewhere she's still standing, folding shirts, slacks
    and underwear, a Virginia Slim centering her mouth,
    and Johnny Mathis on the radio.
The beds are all made, the rooms all empty, and her pillow
    on the arm of the sofa creased and waiting.

I am half certain even now that someone
    is coming with a key that will fit the lock.

The cell block continues sleeping
    with its dreams of other mothers
    busy with perfection, cooking, washing,
    folding clothes for every forgotten child
    whose fingers reach through steel bars
    for dreams destined to fall short.

The sheep go on being counted
in a confused corner of the world
that bears no resemblance to either clouds or prisons.
Still, there will be those who look to the stars as they
take their jittery place on the stage
and the sheepdog prepares for a triumph
he'd thought would never come.

CHAPEL

The storm bloomed overhead, the blue
  darkening with each shiver of thunder, the white
  undertow of wind speeding forward, yoking light
  to a scream.
He leaned into the foliated concretion of rain and
  dust spitting the first notes
  for the coming production
He would learn this summer song, its impartial,
  inhuman rage and name the blinding deafness,
  the silence within the lightning, the roaring
  within the chapel where the peace is passed
  between careless generations of mice
  busy with the nonchalance of natural selection.

TINNITUS

It was in the back orchard I fell
    reaching for a *Wolf River* apple,
    sun-crowned with peach-pink cheeks.
Nothing but the air to fall
    through, the sky turning
    away, and I lay there without tears,
    just looking around for my breath
    and the apple clenched in my fist.
Under my jaw, the scar, a small worm of flesh.
It was my first boon from the long land of memory
    where screams drowned the night,
    then receded with the stitch-work
    of the mysterious elders and their stories,
    stories like a skin within which I could hide, a skin
    wedded seamlessly to my nightshirt
    that I could pull on over my head and so,
    on lucky nights, disappear and go deaf
    with only this ringing, as an old man,
    reminding me of what I've shut out
    and from which I'm still running, still falling,
    fists clenched, but the sky, the sky turning
    its cheek now, slowly, at last, towards me.

ASTONISHED

From my second-story window I watch
   the purpling black band push
   below the white surf of cloud
   a rolling, distant murmur
   following behind.

A bowl of gentians on the window sill
   are speechless.
The mockingbird mocks.
A boy wandered across the lawn earlier
   looking for a ball with his beagle.
I need some help myself, I think.

What's lost in the dry months gets found
   only with a kind of random serendipity:
   loose change in a cup, a flyer
   on the end table advertising hearing-aids,
   a single book of matches.
It's been decades since I've smoked.
I'd not planned to stay. I know that.
And yet here I am settled
   at the same address, at home
   with the familiar losses still
   astonishing me.

FLIGHT BEHAVIOR

There's an autumn wren worrying my feeder,
    though blithely singing as she does so,
    and a blue sky through the stand of hemlocks
    nearly as bright as the sun lighting it
    some ninety-two million miles away.

The wren is a simple creature with a brain
    would fit on my fingertip and yet with wings
    can easily lift her into that sky, that light, closer even
    to that sun than I'll ever get with these heavy arms.

It's all some kind of miracle, I tell myself and,
    though I can't fly, nor sing, nor even balance
    as she does precisely on the delicately fragile and
    thinnest of branches high in that nearest hemlock,
    I do have this brain that imagines her,
    dear wren, dear reader, dear words
    hammered upon white paper, that imagines . . .

That imagines a kind of flight which,
    though it never lift me from earth,
    may lift this moment in which
    that wren hovering at my window
    lifts into view before you
    where you sit

this very minute
reading the continuation
of what, for want of a better word,
I'll go on calling
some kind of miracle.

HAYING

The long stretch of hill field, long hours round
tossing bales into piles, scrambling to keep up
with the baler, dodging yellow jackets sound-
less behind the roar of the tractor, heads up

as well as down, watching for groundhog holes,
rocks, snakes, anything might bite or snag
yet we've still to grip, heave, toss, and up the knoll
go following until finished, then trail the zigzag

paths between scattered piles, now lifting
to fill the wagon, one up, one down, artists
of balance: both to keep the bales from shifting
on the steep, uneven ground and ourselves smart

enough to do the same, stay upright and sure
that when comes the barn all are there, all secure.

POLITICS

Here, on a narrow balcony, the politics have, at last,
       fallen mute.
Hard times ahead, for sure, likely worse, but I believe
       there are moments like now when these geese
       are able to spirit them away, moments
       when even that pale smudge of moon
       holds still its place over the mountain,
            another favor from an avatar
            whose many names I'll never know.
There are, as well, the empty bleachers, and a few crickets
       below them unconcerned with what has gone before,
       and what comes after.
But I do know boys will again "gallop terribly"
       against each other's bodies tonight,
       and when the storytellers take the stage, a girl
       will fall in love with the words *hickory* and *lozenge*.

Believe me, I don't know what to make of any of this,
       but I am inclined to trust the recondite mischief
       of that girl, these random messages
       now flooding over me every day.

Reason is forfeit for this night,
      and my rational fears indicted.
Let me light your cigarette, surrender,
      and then together watch
      this remote country road
      curl into the evening, the silent stream
      carry its sleepy fish below the contented cemetery
      still steady on its bluff, and happy
          to cast its vote for more of the same.

BLUE IN GREEN

It bugs me when people try to analyze jazz as an intellectual
theorem. It's not. It's feeling.

      —Bill Evans

Only a piano, walking bass, and the lightly stepped staccato
      of snare and brush.
Bill Evans.
Blue in Green.
The miles ahead wait under the green light
      of the green haze of the Alleghenies
      whose feet blaze with redbud and early mustard
      somewhere east of Cumberland.
It's feeling, he said.
That's what matters.
And for me, here on the swift black road with the white lines,
      escaping noise, escaping the things that bug me,
      I forego analysis,
      and hearing your piano find feeling,
      look for words to do the same.
Looking for words that do the same . . .
      and suddenly I have a green feeling to turn off
      onto some deserted back country lane

and go lose myself in green, deep green,
forever green,
with just that broken sliver of blue
where the light gets in
and makes me feel.

GRANDMOTHER LOVED TO DANCE

I come here often and find all the same: the erratic breeze,
  the broken sunlight, the open window, the unmade bed.
A postcard from a forgotten year leans against the mantle,
  threatening and observant.
A calendar hangs from a nail in the kitchen
  where the slow ticking of days continues unchanged.
Something fetid in a Mason jar scents the cupboard
  on whose floor the secret messages the mice drop
  remain unread.
Death goes on changing partners even as the clouds
  knit the forested horizon with purple threads
  left over from an earlier sky.
The bronze lamp has begun to green though it still stands
  watch by that easy chair where mysteries
  were eaten like candy: *better than whiskey*
  or sleeping pills.
She held on to more mysteries than those in her paperbacks
  but I never learned their clues
  any more than I ever learned to dance.

LATE OCTOBER

The leaves have by now drifted into closer conversations,
  some wreathing their parents, others snug
  along the curbside.
If it's quiet and the wind stirs, I hear
  their busy whispers come like new rain
  or rattle seditiously, couriers of brittle static.
The silent spiders have been close overhead, stringing
  without effort their delicate transparencies
  through the iron sky that steadily lowers
  itself into the graying forest.
Elsewhere the ground is large-pebbled with walnuts,
  green mottled with the black, best fruit
  of the dying year. The squirrels know.
And, if I'm here long enough, and hold still, I hear
  within myself the echoing ghosts of kinships
  gone too long unnoticed.

SKELETAL

At dusk the mullioned window
       suddenly refracts an alien sky
       across the harlequin floor
       with a dozen rose-rust suns.

You strike a match for the lamp.
The phosphorus tip billows and,
       as you lift the empty teacup,
       you see your fingers
       through the fine bone
       of china.

You take this in stride, this unexpected prefiguring
       of the skeletal life
       that's always followed
       these little moments of beauty
       when confession was forgiven
       and murder almost forgotten.

BEAUTY AND . . .

An old farm, idyllic, ramshackled, rusted gates,
     and tangled garden.
The beans painted with frost
     are dressed for death.
The ivy has gone scarlet
     climbing its way into the sky.
When the landscape painter comes tomorrow,
     he'll have beauty on his mind.
A doe going gray with October
     will watch, motionless,
     rooted like the forest
     within which it stands.
A long-shadowed hawk will scream.
There'll be a scurrying in the leaves:
     chipmunk or vole.

Long ago, two hunters with ancient bloodlines
     squatted here around a fire.
They had venison, beans,
     and their own secret words for beauty,
     and for death enough respect
     to let it stand among their gods.
They shared dreams, one each:
     I can't begin to imagine.

Last night I dreamed a squirrel climbed

> that red tree and told a story
> of a pair of hunters sharing dreams,
> dreams they followed into a future
> that now falls around my shoulders
> like a cobweb
> pebbled with the dead,
> dew-dropped with beauty.

I open my book, open the sky, look around

> for beauty and its twin.

Falling out of the sky, as if to answer me,

> is a sharp-shinned hawk
> who tears a vole
> from its nest of leaves
> and then's off again into a life different from my own
> yet ruled by the same twin poles
> in those dreams I keep having about now, about then,
> about next.

THIRD

A BREACH

We are engaged in a great civil war
over the future of the land
upon which this nation of varied peoples stand,
of the land that has up to now nourished
and nurtured the people who
borrow from it their sustenance.

> —Anonymous

Open now the crystal fountain,
Whence the healing stream doth flow.

> —William Williams, 1717–1791

THROUGH A LITTLE HOLE

I

It's been hand-signals, shouts all afternoon but now Roy
lets in the clutch, turns the key, and the whirring slap
of the Allis Chalmers' idle is stilled. I can hardly see for
the sweat, brush the chaff from my sleeve, and drag the
flannel across my face. I notice Roy lift his cap to do the
same.

The sudden silence is godly. Thunderclouds are lifting
in the west.

Good thing we got her done.

I nod my head—too whipped to speak: three hundred
bales, two men, and this last sixty yet to get to the barn
and into the mow.

Roy's eighty-two, but he slips off the metal seat like a
teenager and lopes toward the trees below the far side of
the knoll. His back to me, he lifts a hand for me to follow.
Though I didn't think I could move, I tramp behind him
several hundred yards into the shade but even here it's
still hot—ninety degrees forecast—perfect for hay but
takes it out of you. I'd hayed with Roy several summers
but never this back field off the point.

Though we descend lower along the hill, we're not
headed for the run. Eventually, he stops: *Listen.* And
when the cicada overhead cuts its droning screed, I hear

it, a steady, small splashing onto stone and, ducking under a tangle of briars, there's the spring flowing out of its metal pipe. I learn later Roy's dad set it half a century ago into this mossy sandstone bank our path had skirted these last few minutes. Looped over a sycamore branch hangs a single, blue enamel cup. Roy's bony, bronze hand slips it off, fills it, and hands it to me—holy hell, is it ever cold . . . I have to sip to keep it from numbing my teeth. But . . . my lovely Jesus—how can water be this sweet?

For the first time in hours, I cool off and, handing the cup back to Roy, slip down, my back against the uneven bank and feel my shoulders loosen, and I breathe. We sit like this for a little eternity, lulled by the sound of this liquid God-gift, crystal-pure, raw-perfect and sacred water . . . I will remember this. Even hours later, scratchy, throwing that last bale into the dark corner of the dusty mow, I will remember and know my thirst was slaked . . . by water pouring free through a little hole in a pipe, through a little hole in the earth.

ANNOTATED TIMELINE FOR "A ONE INCH HOLE"

II

January 9, 2014 [near Charleston, West Virginia]

Early—*A one inch hole* begins leaking hazardous MCHM, from Freedom Industries' chemical storage tank into the soil, then into the Elk River, and then into the WV American Water intake system that supplies water for 300,000 West Virginians. Into them, too, this poison flows. . . . There is a *breach* in the system.
Thousands are drinking morning coffee.

8:15 a.m.—Odor complaints to the WV Department of Environmental Protection.
Children are drinking water, brushing teeth.

11:10 a.m.—The Department of Environmental Protection three hours later travels six point four miles and arrives at Freedom Industries. MCHM identified.
Families, businesses, cafeterias, chefs are washing dishes, preparing foods, setting glasses of water upon tables.

12 noon—WV American Water is aware of spill but assume their filters can manage.
School children in nine counties are drinking from water fountains.

4 p.m.—WVAW realizes filter system won't be able to handle spill.
Parents are preparing dinner, washing clothes, drinking, and bathing.

5:09—WVAW reports water problem.
Pregnant mothers are washing and drinking, young mothers nursing and feeding.

5:45—WVAW advises customers not to drink water.
Everyone until this minute has been drinking, bathing, washing, and will continue to do so until this news filters down to them.

9:32—Governor declares *state of emergency* and advises residents: to "continue to refrain from using the water for drinking, cooking, cleaning, bathing and washing."
Disingenuous or simply . . . too little too late?

January 11—"This was not a coal company incident. This was a chemical company incident." Gov. Earl Ray Tomblin
MCHM's primary, if only, use in the world is as a cleaning agent for washing coal.

January 13—Water declared safe to drink.
Pregnant mothers resume washing and drinking, other mothers their nursing and feeding.

January 15—CDC urges pregnant women not to use the water. *What the fuck?*

January 19—A special meeting in the governor's chambers. Invited are the WV Chamber of Commerce, the Oil and Gas Association, and the WV Coal Association. Their task is to design recommendations for legislation regarding future accidents.
Where the voices of the innocent? Where any voice but vested corporate interests?

February 2—from *The Guardian*, London, England ". . . the coal industry [in WV] has spent upward of $14m a year for the past four years on lobbying efforts, not including the $14m they spent [just] last year on direct contributions to campaigns."

Mary Harris "Mother" Jones: "I believe that [none] who hold [leadership positions] should ever accept favors from either side. [They] are then committed to show favors."

* * * *

This is a breach in governance, the belief
      in a *government of the people, by the people,*
         for the people . . .
There are holes in the language
      where the lies creep in, holes
      in pipes where the poison flows, holes
      in the logic that looks the other way.

DREAMS ENTER THROUGH A HOLE IN MY HEAD

III

Restless night, woke in a sweat, slipped on shoes, jeans, t-shirt, went out, ducked below the pines, and walked up the pasture. The moon, lifting over Pleasant Ridge, full and sun-brilliant, shadows sharp and . . . then there was Jesus standing with the woman at the well. Desert-dry, and I was sweating again. He turned full to face me, the empty bucket at his feet, upturned, the well . . . dry, and he lifted his hands to me. They were bleeding. There were already holes in his palms, as time and place shifted. There was no living water to keep the universe right and the woman, she turned to me, her clothes slashed, torn. She was bruised and cut all over, breasts bare, purple with angry welts. She'd been stoned. Which woman was she? But then I knew it didn't matter, mercy had been stoned. She'd been stoned for all her trouble. She'd been stoned for trying to tell the truth about living water. She turns to me, her lips cracked, voice a ragged whisper: ". . . in our father Jacob's well, not one drop left, not even for the Messiah . . . no living water . . . ?"

I walked on and before me rose a great lake with a smell of rot upon it, dead fish, and animals and people, and licorice, and there was Jesus again, this time with those undependable fishermen, those low-life friends of his. But they'd tried, you could tell, by all their nets and the sweat streaming from their faces, or were they tears? And here was Jesus bleeding again, big holes in his feet. He could hardly stand. And now behind me I saw crowds of people, my people, the people of these mountains, and they were gathering, wailing, carrying sick children, people with rashes and throat fires and cancers and death and they were thirsty, so thirsty, and *one of the least of these* fishermen friends comes to me, weeping, and asks: *how shall we feed them, how heal so many of so much, how slake a thirst such as this?*

And somewhere north of here there were tick tankers and pipe-liners, the sand cans and brine trucks, out-of-state corporations and out-of-state workers daily threading a new slurry of poisons into earth and ancient water to lift prehistoric gas out of prehistoric rock all for profit and little enough for us who live here. It's called fracking.

THERE'S A HOLE IN THEIR ARGUMENTS . . .

IV

Economy?

Huge new shipping facilities built along the coasts to ship overseas and so goes the argument about alleviating fuel shortages in the USA.

Jobs?

Job growth in the industry has been greatest (as a share of total employment) in West Virginia. Still, shale-related employment is less than 2 percent of total West Virginia employment and less than half a percent of total employment in all the other states.

Environment?

Lift this cup to your lips, taste and see: Benzene, Ethylbenzene, Toulene, Xylene, Naphthalene, Polycyclic Aromatic Hydrocarbons, Methanol, Formaldehyde, Ethylene glycol, Glycol ethers, Hydrochloric acid, Sodium Hydroxide, C8, diesel fuel . . .

Changes?

Murder. Prostitution. Vehicular homicide. Drugs.
Crumbling infrastructure in rural counties. Oh, yes,
groundwater contamination, the living water too fouled
to drink, to bathe. But these little catastrophes rarely
make the national news . . . .

Questions?

Go ask . . . . Chesapeake, Antero, Dominion Energy,
Stonewall Gas Gathering, LLC, Consol Energy, MarkWest,
EQT, Trans Energy, Jay-Bee Oil and Gas, East Resources,
Range Resources, Southwestern Energy Co, Williams
Companies, Baker Hughes, DuPont, Schlumberger, . . .
Halliburton.

Go ask if there's anything trumps profit? This simple
question answers all others. That *anything* includes
increased unemployment; species extinction; murder;
prostitution; increased drug use; increased automotive
violence; infrastructure collapse; flaming faucets;
blackened water; poisoning of wildlife, cattle, children.

THE HOLE THAT REMEMBERS AN ANCIENT WELL

V

"How slake such a thirst?"

I couldn't stay and walked away, and minutes into hours later suddenly there was more water, a great sea, and there was Jesus again, setting out to walk those waters, to calm the storming waves, but then there were no waves, there was no storm, the disaster had already come and gone. There was no sea. Everywhere was dry, dry sand. It was the valley of dry bones, thousands and thousands of them, and Jesus wept for these uncounted numbers of Lazarus-dead, and the twelve wept, and Mary wept, and Lazarus wept, and myself, and everyone I knew wept for how could even Jesus with his hands so bloodied and mangled ever begin to knit flesh and sinew back into these bones, how fix, how especially if there was no water to cleanse those wounds, to mop his sweet face, how when there was only bile and vinegar and licorice water, how to do all this without . . . without living water?

You shall not pollute the land in which you live, [. . .] You shall not defile the land in which you live, in the midst of which I dwell, for I the Lord dwell in the midst of the people of Israel.

— Numbers 35:33–34 ESV

OTHER HOLES IN THE GROUND

VI

—"Marcellus Miracle to Save the Economy"

Is it just the moon flaring
    behind the jagged silhouette of the ridgeline?
He is alone in the deep cliff-cut
    of the stream, shadow-less
    and wary—only the stream talking.
He's seen enough this past year:
    the wrecks, paved roads become dirt,
    Orma's dog, Finley's garden,
    his own mailbox . . .
Forget compensation—find a lawyer,
    and before you know it things go
    missing around the farm,
    your wife gets anonymous threats. Coincidences?
Or that college boy murdered in Wheeling, or the two
    women crushed in their car
    by fracking pipe rolling off truck.
Just an *accident*. And not the fracking industry.

    The drivers were *"ancillary workers."*

Vera Scroggins, unarmed but for words and silver hair, is
banned from setting foot on 312.5 square miles of northeast
Appalachian Pennsylvania. Gag orders are placed on children,

requiring they never speak about Range Resources and what
went on around Mount Pleasant, Pennsylvania, in 2011.

When the drill rigs came for the new gas
      every one was asleep
      with their eyes open
      and times were tough and money talked
      more persuasively than any stream.
So, tonight he's standing beside the noisy stream,
      not sleeping but watching.

He wants to see, to see what they're doing up there now.
Is it another screw-up, flames not moon-light, a flare-out
      or spill that's found a cigarette, a spark?

When you can't see the forest, can't see the trees,
      well, *you don't miss your water till your well runs . . .*
      dry or black, flames or poison.
Brookies lived in those pools on Lower Bowman,
      a night sky so brilliant with dark the stars pulsed
      in tune with living hearts.
The Chesapeake glare destroys the night
      and the 24/7 roar destroys the day.

We had the best well water in the county,
      cold and pure as any spring.

A FEW SENTENCES THREADING THE HOLES TOGETHER

VII

I've stood in the midnight wilderness and seen it
 lit daylight bright with well rigs.
I've seen the road wind in and out along the orange stream
 below the mountain.
I've seen the gray and brown waste smoking
 with dust under summer's sun.
I've seen where the cemetery was shoveled
 over the side of the hill.
I've seen the bullet holes and graffiti
 on Larry's outbuildings.
I've also seen a piece of fuse I picked up
 on Kayford Mountain.
I've stood in a hotel room listening to a lovely woman
 telling me not to drink the water.
I've walked a sidewalk where a young man was murdered
 because an out-of-state worker
 had enough of a crap job and enough beer
 to light his fuse.
I've seen gas and coal drive unemployment up
 and property prices down.

I've seen enough that no politician can ever lie to me again
about how it's all about jobs,
how it's war on coal, how it's the EPA, how it's not his
fault, how it's not poetry, how
it is . . .

A SMALL HOLE WHERE A LAST POEM ENTERS

VIII

A cold, steady flow
     unseen and
     splattering upon soft stone,
     goes where it will
     down the hill and away.
Chances were good, once,
     under the unbroken shade
     of the Alleghenies
     that it might've found itself joined, here, there,
     and with every joining increase
     into stream, river, and
     finally sea, the great path's destination
     to brew the rain, to slake the all-thirst
     that drives us all living, alive, filled
     with waters not marred by the hand of men.

FOURTH

HEART WORK

Straight shafts of shadow gone crooked
      with the imprint of the trees that bore them:
      the hillside threatens to collapse under their weight.

The neighbor's mower is busy shaving his lawn—
      the buzzing constant.
I can't understand what it's saying.

There is so much getting said some days
      that it's hard to keep anything straight.
What was crooked to begin with?
A man's heart.
The sharp blades of steel.
The innocence of grass.

Strong fingers of shadow reach down the hillside
      and strangle the noise, the words caught there.
They are dreams thick with promises.
I count them, and lift them up.
Suddenly, the world is lighter and the trees
      disappear like my fingers do
      when the light goes out and
      they're still tapping a rhythm
      that remembers how the crooked
      was to be made straight.

JUST OUTSIDE THE GROCERY A BOY
WITH A GUN

The memory still pulses some days like the minutes
      held inside his trembling fist.

The rutabagas are still on sale below where
      the six-packs stand sentinel at the far end of the aisle.

Outside the blood's gone brown beside the traffic cone
      and will eventually bleach with the sun
      and go unnoticed even by the drunk
      who studies the pavement for change.

Grief climbed into that ambulance
      along with the paramedicsand crossed the night river
      in silence even as the moon placed its crown
      over top of the mountain.

The cashier was installing a new paper roll.

Security was helping grandma pick up
      her spilled juice bottle.

The manager was mismanaging his iPhone flirtation
      with increasing mumbles and curses.

The boy had not intended to pull the gun,
    let alone the trigger,
    but she'd said something he thought he didn't like
    and there was so much he didn't like these days.

He was sure she must have said just that thing
    but with the recoil, the sharp, short shot, the blood,
    her surprisingly innocent last look the air cleared
    and all he could hear was simply
    please, please, please . . . please.

APRIL 17, ROMNEY ROAD

The sun is framed in the hemlock,
      a palette of green shadows and whatever
      impossible word stands in for the dazzling light,
      and the branches, a chiaroscuro
      they've helped perfect and done so without paint.

Myself, I'm trying to take some account
      for the day within, to align memory
      with something more than time,
      its requisite weather of responsibilities.

These, then: a wide smear of blood on the highway,
      the undulating swoop and glide of a woodpecker,
      the white violets who've increased their hold
      on one corner of the lawn, and today's new name
      from the poor, the young sacrificed to guns and pride.

What's left is the ring of a bell somewhere
      deeper in the village, an echoing
      slowly going under the rising surf
      of the evening's chorus of birds and insects and frogs.

I would sing this if I could,
          teach it if I believed I knew,
          and preach it if I believed I believed.

Surrender, then, I must, trusting
          some kind of grace to deliver me
          to something somehow more.

NOT A BOY SCOUT

The April evening comes with a gust of wind
     and a sudden slash of sunlight.
The bus has left a lingering perfume of diesel.
Shift change.
A siren threads the southern valley.
In the quiet afterwards the monotonous exchange
     of *coos* from a pair of doves.
About the knuckled roots of the ancient oak
     an embrace of bluebells.
I must tell her soon what the doctor said to expect.
Green dots speckle the black garden—the promise of lettuce.
To everything there must be something
     like a season impatiently waiting for its cue.
On my walk I found: a bottle cap, several acorns, a used
     rubber, a doll-sized buggy, and enough twigs
     for kindling should the temperature continue to fall.
I was never a boy scout but even I know their motto
     and trust it to be as good as scripture.

SURRENDER

Pinned to the breast of the hill, a pair of daffodils,
    a living brooch, and within
    twin bees busy working for honey.
April, and a spider of bare branches
    is still framing the swift sky overhead.
Below, a grackle's mechanical pacing
    of the minutes left within this poem
    have called me to attention.
Constable's clouds are singing
    the dark songs of Hampstead and Keats
    . . . save what from heaven is with the breezes blown . . .
How do I know this is so?
A poet told me.
How else do we learn anything that matters?
I grab a fistful of coins and fling them
    onto the sloping lawn
    where they catch the sun
    like the eyes of Cinderella's silver mice.
All goes on and outwards, even the stories.
The only flag to raise in the midst of all this
    is the white flag—you know the one.

NOWHERE BEYOND

A fading sun was leaning on the blue snow
      tracked and printed with the day's wild travelers
      though as yet none of my own.

Silent, that stiff page, until my boots crack
      its skin, crunch through February's layered crust,
      thin echoes following
    without any sense of companionship.

It stretched as far away as childhood this path
      that led nowhere beyond itself and the edge
      of the falling night and a far pasture-line
      of trees and the deeper shadows within.

Death could be between us, between those
      whose litter of markings I'd pretended
      to understand, as if the palimpsest map
      white and innocent beneath me
      could show where I needed to go.

Morning could come and fresh snow
      settle—an erasure within the night—
      capturing me as easily as the come and go
      of these wild ones, knowing nothing
      of nowhere but how to move beyond.

THE NEWS AND THE HISTORY

But of that day and hour no one knows, not even
the angels of heaven . . .

   —Matthew 24:36 ff.

So not news, not exactly, this
  newest suffering
  of the suffering.
And like the needle in the haystack
  the angels will be hard to find
  unless you count
  neighbor and kin.

And the rains come and the mountains shift
  enough, enough
  to show they're watching.

Listen.
There's nothing like the roar of water with
  no place to go.
There's nothing like the roar of water
  when you yourself have
  no place to go.

Watch that green field slowly become
  a brown smear almost innocent.
Watch the buildings jockey for position
  in the out-rush to destruction.

Watch the skies empty their bowels
      hour after hour after hour.

What of the history?
Where's that in the headlines?
What of those clear cuts, the strip mines,
      the fracking roads, the MTR?

A lot of people are angry. Even more weep.

I want to hear the preachers preach justice,
      I want to see tears and anger turn
      to justice.
I want to hear the politicians
      put up or shut up, as Father liked to say,
      I want to see their hands in the mud, see
      a light bulb finally flash when the history
      comes clear, their co-operation exposed
      for what it is.

What's happening here is happening elsewhere.
This is not poetry.
This is not even news.
This is you. This is me.
This is a life getting turned upside down.
These are buildings and bridges, homes and businesses
      wet through, molding, rotting, lost.

These are precious books, scores, banjos and fiddles ruined.
These are lessons delayed, bills continuing,
      Christmases postponed.
These are lives lost.
This is someone drowned, pulled under,
      gone, gone, . . . gone.
This is not forgettable, forgivable, not easily explained
      as if just another headline, another banner
      streaming and running
      below the weather channel's pretty maps.
This is life broken, cascading under a broken bridge and
      looking to all the world as if it's just trash, junk
      when it was once all and more
      of a life, a life, lives
      lived under a more benevolent sky, lives lived
      in hope that justice might begin to stitch
      these mountains back together, might begin
      to ascend the statehouse steps and march
      back down with something more than
      meager compensation, false hope, lies
      that it won't happen again, won't become
      just another headline, more forgotten history.

REMINDERS

A squirrel is loping the high wire
>over Main Street, Elkins, West Virginia.

A purple hairstreak meanders about a mistletoe
>slumbering in an elm.

And me, I'm following a coal truck
>disgorging black smoke as I head north.

I swear: *Goddamn it.*

Then, slower, think
>that it is what it is, a small town in Appalachia.

And weren't you and I just in full voice, no worries, singing?
No?

Still we were *in* something as fluent as singing, as song,
>a fluent conversation about Coltrane, let's say,

>or Ravel, string bands, first beers,

>first kisses, first deaths—fluently reminding ourselves

>that reminding ourselves is what we do

>that makes this singing sing.

A block further out, the song continues
>along the overgrown bank

>where, in their formal attire, the men in orange suits

>are shoving their lawnmowers, lifting the perfect smell

>of new mown grass—bless them.

They should get a day, no, a week, a year off their sentences.
The clouds run in rivers overhead.

The sky is open for the business of glory, and poetry,
    and eternity.
Who else arranged this but these dedicated men
    dressed for respectable work?
What else but this squirrel out on a frolic,
    that butterfly reconnoitering?
Who else but you and I who've reminded ourselves
    to look for them doing *this*, what else but friendship,
    how else but by doing the work,

    rifling the word hoard
    for a chance to see again, and sing,

    sing, perhaps, this song
    for this small town in the lost mountains

    of this deranged country,
    sing, and so take our refuge where we can, if not

    in the gods, at least in these, the little men,

    the little butterflies, the little squirrels,
    all doing what they do, perhaps, even,

    all any of us ever can.

THE END

NOTES

Well Enough—The echo of "all will be well" from Julian of Norwich's (1343–1416) famous lines is intentional; these words are also used by T. S. Eliot in the final stanza of the "Little Gidding" section of *Four Quartets*. Julian of Norwich: "All shall be well, and all shall be well and all manner of thing shall be well."

Flight Behavior—The poem's title is inspired by the novel *Flight Behavior: A Novel* by Barbara Kingsolver (Harper, NY, 2012).

Politics—The quotation in the 11th line comes from the poem "Autumn Begins in Martins Ferry, Ohio" by James Wright.

Blue in Green—The tune "Blue in Green" is the famous, and controversial third track on the legendary *Kind of Blue* album by Miles Davis. Although Davis takes credit for composing it, most consider it to have been Evans's creation from the beginning. Here, I have in mind the version on the album *Portrait in Jazz* recorded eight months after *Kind of Blue*, where Evans heads his own trio with Scott LaFaro on bass and Paul Motian on drums. The credit there is listed as Davis/Evans.

A Breach—Source for stanzas 4 and 6: "Coal River Mountain Watch, Ohio Policy Matters, Appalachian Voices, West Virginia Highlands Conservancy." The line in section five that reads "you don't miss your water till your well runs dry" is an echo from the soul song "You Don't Miss Your Water," written by William Bell (1961) and covered in 1965 by Otis Redding.

Surrender—The quotation in line 11 is from "Ode to a Nightingale" by John Keats.

ABOUT THE AUTHOR

Marc Harshman, besides being a poet, is the author of 14 nationally acclaimed children's books, including *Fallingwater: The Building of Frank Lloyd Wright's Masterpiece*, co-authored with Anna Egan Smucker, illustrated by LeUyen Pham, and subsequently named an Amazon Book of the Month. Previous titles have included *The Storm*, a Smithsonian Notable Book. His children's books have been published in Spanish, Korean, Danish, Japanese, and Swedish. His collections of poetry include *Woman in Red Anorak*, winner of the Blue Lynx Prize, and *Believe What You Can*, winner of the Weatherford Award from the Appalachian Studies Association (Vandalia/WVU Press) and also named the Appalachian Book of the Year by the Mountain Heritage Literary Festival in Tennessee. *Dark Hills of Home* was published by Monongahela Book in 2022 to celebrate Harshman's 10th anniversary as WV Poet Laureate, and his latest volume is *Following the Silence* from Press 53. Harshman was recently named the Appalachian Heritage Writer for 2024 by Shepherd University's Appalachian Studies program, whose past honorees have included Barbara Kingsolver, Charles Frazier, Bobbie Ann Mason, Henry Louis Gates, and Nikki Giovanni. He is co-winner of the Allen Ginsberg Poetry Award, and his poem "Dispatch from the Mountain State" appeared in the 2020 Thanksgiving edition of the *New York Times*. He holds degrees from Bethany College, Yale University Divinity School, and the University of Pittsburgh. Appointed in 2012 by Governor Earl Ray Tomblin, Harshman is the seventh poet laureate of West Virginia.